Bath St

a quarry history

by
J. W. PERKINS, A. T. BROOKS &
A. E. McR. PEARCE

Published by the Department of Extra-mural Studies
University College Cardiff

First printed 1979 (under ISBN 0 906230 26 8)

Reprinted 1983 and 1990

ISBN 0 946045 24 0

Text set in 10/12 pt VIP Century Roman, printed and bound in Great Britain at The Bath Press, Avon

FOREWORD

Bath Stone rightly holds a place of fame among the leading English building stones. It has certainly been worked for nearly 2,000 years since there are Roman buildings constructed of it, some of them still in use today. Surprisingly little has been written on the working of the stone, but there is much about the history of Bath itself, of the people who lived there, and so on. One or two items in local caving club journals cover the old mines from that viewpoint. The Bath Stone mines contracted in number after the Second War, and have been mechanised since 1948, so it seems to the present writers that some record of the working of Bath Stone is timely and, in the case of the older methods, particularly urgent.

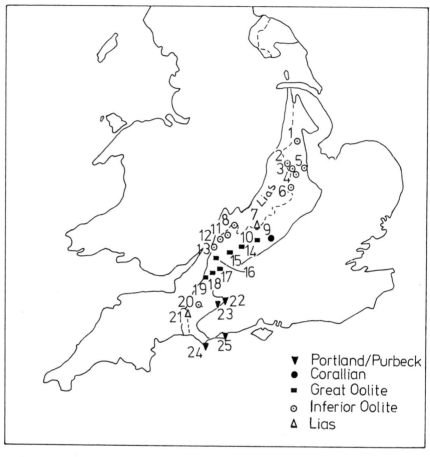

1	Ancaster	10	Stonesfield (slates)	19	Bath
2	Clipsham	11	Guiting	20	Doulting
3	Ketton	12	Leckhampton	21	Ham Hill
4	Collyweston (slates)	13	Painswick	22	Tisbury
5	Barnack	14	Taynton	23	Chilmark
6	Weldon	15	Cirencester	24	Portland
7	Hornton	16	Minchinhampton	25	Purbeck
8	Chipping Camden	17	Corsham		
9	Headington	18	Box		

Fig. 1. Some Jurassic Building Stones of England.

ORIGINS

The skills of the mason and the architect are readily seen in many beautiful buildings, but the many chance events of the earth's history which have given us this beautiful golden stone are less well known. Bath Stone is an oolitic limestone—made of grain-like fragments of calcium carbonate which resemble a fish roe in appearance. Each little grain became coated with lime as it was rolled around on the sea bed. When highly magnified, the centres of the grains or ooliths often reveal small shell or rock fragments around which the coating accumulated. Where was this sea-bed and when did all this take place?

The origins of Bath Stone involve a journey through time to a period of the earth's history about 200 million years ago. Neither Bath nor the British Isles existed as such in those days but the names must be used for convenience in telling the geological story. At that far off time the continents of the world were grouped in one great land-mass which geologists call Pangea. This great supercontinent straddled the Equator and Britain was locked in its arid interior, roughly in the latitudes of the present Sahara desert, a region of semi-arid climate with red marls and sandstones forming in dunes, temporary lake and flash flood conditions. The rocks of those times are known as the Permo-Triassic. Surviving outcrops of them can be seen along the Teignmouth-Budleigh Salterton coast in Devon or at Aust and other cliffs around the Severn Estuary.

About 190 million years ago the great continent began to break up. Its fragments gradually moved apart to their present positions. Europe and the British Isles drifted north with Africa following, and occasionally shunting into southern Europe, while North and South America moved off westwards. This disintegration of Pangea allowed the sea to invade its heartland and eventually lead to the creation of the Atlantic Ocean. The earlier red desert rocks were covered by marine sediments in a new period of geological time called the Jurassic, which lasted from 195 to 135 million years ago and saw

Britain drift from latitude 30°N to 40°N.

The Jurassic seas which submerged Pangea did so in a series of basins, constantly changing and subsiding though never very deep. Here the rocks, of which Bath Stone is a part, were born—a great variety of limestone, sandstones and clays.

Many events have taken place in the geological history of Britain since those far off days but three are important in the history of Bath Stone. Firstly, the British Isles and Europe continued to drift northwards to our present latitude and secondly, about 25 million years ago, during one of Africa's shunting movements the mountain chains of southern Europe were formed while the Jurassic beds of Britain were tilted into a gently southeastward sloping attitude. Running across the geological map of England from Purbeck and Portland in the south, through Bath, the Cotswolds, Northamptonshire and Lincolnshire, to the North York Moors, the Jurassic outcrop is the visible rim of this southeast dipping sequence. Good building stones occur at many places along this outcrop and the Jurassic is one of Britain's most prolific formations for building stones. Geologists subdivide the rocks of the Jurassic as follows:

JURASSIC
- Purbeck Beds
- Portland Beds
- Kimmeridge Clay
- Corallian Beds
- Oxford Clay
- Forest Marble
- Great Oolite
- Fullers Earth
- Inferior Oolite (in the sense of lower)
- Upper Lias
- Middle Lias
- Lower Lias

N.B. the geological convention of giving the oldest i.e. first formed beds at the base, the youngest at the top.

Bath Stone belongs to the Great Oolite, which further subdivides into:

Bradford Clay
Upper Rags (including Bradford Coral Bed, Ancliff Oolite and Corsham Coral Bed)

Bath Oolite

Twinhoe Beds
{ Winsley facies
Freshford facies
Twinhoe ironshot facies
Combe Down Oolite

The third important geological event to take place since the formation of Bath Stone was the creation of the present Avon river system. Cutting through the southeast sloping sequence, this valley is the key to the way Bath Stone has been worked at various localities. Around the city itself the stone beds are high in the hill tops, giving the latter much of their plateau-like character and close enough to the surface to be obtained from opencast pits, e.g. Combe Down, Odd Down. The Romans worked these near city areas and as they mined as well would have only had very shallow depths to contend with.

To the east, i.e. further up the Avon, plateau-like hilltops continue, but their southeasterly slope is at a slightly lower angle than the rock beds, so beds which lie higher in the succession than the useful stone now form the plateau surface. The valuable material lies a little below hill top level around Monkton Farleigh, Conkwell, Winsley and Box for example. In these districts the Avon provided many hillside exposures which were worked in long outcrop quarries and then, where the quality was good as at Box, mining followed, pursuing the beds in under the hilltop capping.

Finally, by the time the most easterly workings around Corsham are reached the difference between the dip of the land surface and that of the rocks places the useful stone beds about 90 feet below the surface. At that depth opencast working has always been uneconomic and all working has been by mining.

In these more easterly areas one of the beds in the overlying sequence becomes very important—the Bradford Clay (see succession, above). Worked at Bradford on Avon by the famous early geologist and canal engineer William Smith as a puddling clay during construction of the Kennet and Avon canal, this layer acts as a waterproofing horizon for the stone mines. Water descending from the surface is diverted away through the rocks along the top of this impervious bed, keeping the stone mines relatively dry.

Perhaps a stone working tradition should be mentioned at this point. The terms opencast quarry and mine are used for clarity in many parts of this booklet, but to the older stone worker all places where stone was dug were quarries, whether above or below ground no distinction was made. Hence the title of this booklet, even though its purpose is largely to illustrate stone mines!

Several important characteristics of Bath Stone also stem from its geological history. The oolitic texture has already been described but being a sedimentary rock it also has a natural layering or bedding (original horizontal partings in the rock) and vertical breaks or joints. Bedding is formed at the time of deposition but jointing is more the result of subsequent folding of rocks. Fortunately, as described, the Jurassic beds have only been gently tilted and joints are not as numerous as they would be with more severe folding or in a different rock type.

A major feature of the stone is that it is a freestone, that is, one which can be sawn or squared up in any direction, quite independently of the alignment of the joints. While the joints do not greatly affect the use of the stone the bedding most certainly does—to obtain satisfactory results and wear Bath Stone must be 'laid on its bed', i.e., the same way up in the building as when in the ground.

HISTORY OF WORKING

The Romans were adept at both quarrying and mining. Their baths in Bath and remains of their villas at Box, Colerne, Combe Down and Farleigh provide evidence of the first large scale working of the stone. The sites of this activity have never been accurately located but the quality of their material, sound unweathered stone, shows that much of it must have been mined. The area tentatively identified with their operations is on the south side of Bath near the Foss Way but they must have worked in the Box area as well.

The collapse of the Roman empire in AD 410 left the native inhabitants of Britain to continue the Romanised way of life they had adopted during the occupation. The buildings in Bath were certainly maintained for a while, probably until AD 577 when the Saxons took over the city. Destruction of the Roman way of life followed, accelerating the decay of the existing buildings, but the Saxon period must not be seen as a dark age in the use of Bath Stone. It was still required for monastic houses, defensive walls, etc. Unfortunately the Saxons often took what they needed from former Roman buildings rather than undertake new quarrying. This is an unhappy feature of all stone working history, widespread in both time and place. One result is that it is more than likely that Bath Stone blocks first dug by the Romans have been re-used many times and may still be in use in buildings other than the surviving Roman ones.

The Saxon era, AD 410 to AD 1066, is notable for three reasons in the stone trade. Aubrey, a Wiltshire antiquary of 1626–97, records the tradition that St. Aldhelm (645–709AD) discovered Box Ground Stone. Riding across Hazelbury he threw down his glove and told them to dig there and they should find great treasure—meaning the valuable stone beds. St. Aldhelm founded Malmesbury Abbey and the stone was used in its construction. An important church of the same period is also accredited to him, the seventh century St. Lawrence's at Bradford on Avon. The lower walls are certainly Saxon although the style of the

9

upper parts suggests changes at a later date. It is probably the oldest surviving church in England.

A much larger religious building forms a third feature of the Saxon period. In 781 St. Peter's Abbey was built in Bath, again largely from old reworked Roman stone it seems. In it the Saxon king Edgar (reigned 959–975AD), the first 'king of a united England', was crowned in 973.

Saxon Bath was ravaged in an early Norman rebellion against William II, but a Norman cathedral was built in 1107, probably using stone from both Roman and Saxon remains. Under the direction of John Villula, a former chaplain of the King who obtained appointment as Bishop of Bath, this building was larger than the present abbey. Villula's activities were not entirely at the expense of earlier works however, since he temporarily revived the baths and his son built a church in Holloway just outside the city. The existence of other churches in Norman Bath is proved by the record of two surviving in the early eighteenth century, though all trace of them disappeared soon afterward.

Slow development seems to characterise the years between the Normans and the eighteenth century but this may be more an impression due to shortage of records than a reality. By the fifteenth century the cathedral was in ruins. The present abbey, begun 1499 was incomplete at the dissolution of the monasteries in 1539. In time honoured fashion the corporation are said to have taken stone from the incomplete buildings for the erection of a guildhall in the High Street, reputedly designed by Inigo Jones while on a visit to Bath. It was to last about two hundred years and be demolished in 1777.

In the Box area there are several records for the early part of this period, concerned with grants to four religious houses, Lacock and Stanley Abbeys and the priories at Bradenstoke and Monkton Farleigh. All these concerned Hazelbury. The four houses seem to have rivalled each other in the magnificence of their buildings. Later on the owner of Great Chalfield Manor held quarry land at Hazelbury and also the Thynne family, Marquis of Bath, of Longleat. Other quarries were probably active intermittently in the area for local use, but Hazelbury with the Box Ground variety of stone enjoyed a reputation for the quality needed in major projects.

At the end of the 'quiet' interval, in seventeenth century Bath a number of well-constructed stone houses had been built. They were occupied by medical men who waited on the people coming to take the waters. Pepys noted them on his visit in 1668 when he also walked around the city walls. A walled town with stone houses seems a contradiction to the oft repeated statement that the qualities of Bath Stone were forgotten between Norman times and the eighteenth century—there were other towns nearby using the oolite, e.g. Bradford on Avon. It is more realistic to say that the activity of those centuries only seems negligible because of the enormous fashionable upsurge which was to follow in Bath itself.

If golden Bath Stone has had a golden age then it must be in the eighteenth and nineteenth centuries. The well worn phrase 'the place, the time and the man' certainly applies to this flowering. In 1710 Ralph Allen came to Bath and established himself in the postal business. Bath Stone was in local use at that time, but in 1724–27 the River Avon was made navigable down to Bristol and Allen took the opportunity to establish himself in stone quarrying, working the beds at Combe and Hampton Downs. Allen with his business acumen was lucky to have a partner who had the architectural flair, John Wood. Together they set the scene for fashionable Bath, the stage for Beau Nash to expand upon, and the famous and titled of the land flocked to the beautiful Georgian city to be housed in walls of golden oolite.

The first ten years saw a number of problems to be overcome, transport difficulties and local opposition to development. One vital aspect of the work of Allen and Wood was the installation of a tramway in 1730 from the quarries down to the Avon at Dolemeads wharf. This cut the cost of stone in Bath itself by twenty-five percent, and an engraving of it drawn in 1750 and published in 1752 enjoys the reputation of being the earliest known railway print. Another feature was the construction in 1737 of Allen's own house Prior Park, adjacent to the tramway. Overlooking Bath, it was an advertisement few could miss and one of the earliest mansions of a new breed of landowner, the self-made man. John Wood died in 1754 but his son, also John, carried on developments in Bath. Although Ralph Allen also died ten years later, the golden age did not falter and continued into the next century.

In the nineteenth century there were two further stimuli to the stone quarry trade. The first of these was the opening of the Kennet and Avon canal in 1810, shifting the area of quarrying activity eastwards to up-river sites, e.g. Avoncliff, Conkwell, Dundas and Winsley, some of them connected to the canal by incline planes. The canal now provided cheap transport eastwards to the Swindon area, the Thames valley and particularly the markets of the Oxford colleges and to London. The classic example of poorly selected stone is the canal's own Avoncliff aqueduct, obtained from a quarry worked solely for that purpose in the adjacent valleyside. Notably the parapets which come from lower or underground beds are of much better quality than the rest of the structure.

The second nineteenth century stimulus came from the digging of the Box railway tunnel in 1836–41 for the Great Western Railway. Although worked by the Romans and by St. Aldhelm, it was this tunnel which drew the attention of the stone trade to the reserves and the quality of the Box stone under the hills to the east. The centre of activity once again shifted in that direction and the great era of underground mining between Box and Corsham began. Around the Box tunnel the situation was a classic example of economic mining, the natural eastward dip of the stone beds reaching main railway level near the eastern end of the tunnel. A separate mineral railway into the growing network of mine galleries thus had an all downhill gravity feed for its loaded wagons. By 1864, 100,000 tons of stone per year were being despatched from Corsham station, reaching Birmingham at 1s. 5d. per cubic foot; Plymouth for 1s. 4d.; Newcastle, 1s. 7d. (1s. = 5p). Since the stone only cost 6d. per cubic foot locally, there was little temptation to think of bricks for economy.

1841 Census, Wiltshire	Quarriers 110 Masons/Cutters 1,320
1861	Quarriers 373 (60% of these in Bath Stone trade)
1901	1,199 in the stone trades generally.

The main firms involved in the nineteenth century activity were Job Pictor at Box, Randall & Saunders at Corsham, Farleigh, Murhill and Combe Downs, Sumsions at Combe Down and Monks Park, Corsham. In 1887, with Samuel Noble of Box, Isaac Smith, J. T. F. Turner and R. F. Giles of Bath and George Hancock of Corsham, they amalgamated to form the Bath Stone Firms Ltd. The Pictor family provided the first chairman of the new company. Despite the fact that this amalgamation took place nearly a century ago the various works are still known to the stone quarriers by their original names—Pictor's Monks, Sumsion's Monks, Strong's Quarry etc. One older firm remained independent at the time, The Yockney and Hartham Park

12

Stone Co., but were eventually taken over in 1944.

The First World War did not depress the stone trade very greatly but overseas markets did contract in the inter-war years with the tariff barriers of the U.S.A. during the depression for example. Working of the stone continued by the old hand methods, which were still profitable.

In the Second World War all the underground quarries were requisitioned as storage areas for ammunition etc., with the exception of the long abandoned or flood prone ones, and it was then, with the cessation of production, that the old order's days were numbered. After the war shortage of skilled labour hastened the introduction of mechanisation in which the company was something of a pioneer, spurred on by the demands for repairs to war damaged buildings. Moor Park Quarry was the first works released and quarrying began again

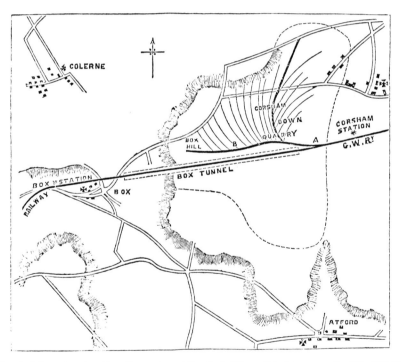

Fig. 2. Map showing Box Tunnel and the Bath Stone Workings under Box Hill. *The Builder*, 1862.

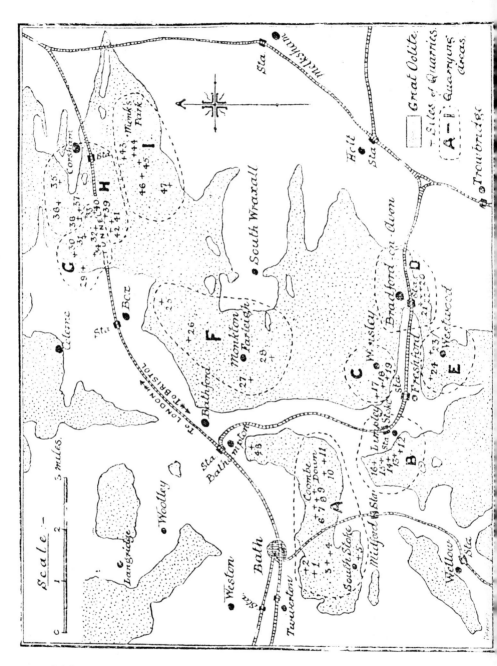

Fig. 3. The Stone Producing Districts & Quarries in 1895. *The Builder*, 1895.

List of districts and quarries (with tentative identifications where only the number was given).

A. Bath area (Odd Down and Combe Down stone).
B. Limpley Stoke area (Stoke Ground stone).
C. Winsley area (Winsley Ground stone).
D. Bradford on Avon area.
E. Westwood area (Westwood Ground stone).
F. Monkton Farleigh area (Farleigh Down stone, Kingsdown).
G. Box area (Box Ground stone).
H. Corsham area (Corsham Down, Corngrit and Hartham Park stones).
I. Monk's Park area (Monk's Park, Ridge, Corsham and Park Lane stones).

All mines unless stated. Article refers to all being mines except one in Box area, those at Winsley, those at Odd Down and the majority at Combe Down. In list here, open means opencast and names in brackets are tentative identifications with later names.

1–6 all open works, no names given (1–5, South Stoke quarries).   7 open, Prior Park quarry.   8–9 open.   10 open, Mount Pleasant quarry.   11 part open, part mine, only mine on Combe Down.   12–16 numbers 13/14 linked underground, possibly to number 15 also (12, Hayeswood; 13–16 Stoke quarries).   17 long open face, Old Murhill, inclined plane to canal.   18–19 open (Winsley).   20 open, close to canal, Woodside quarry.   21–22 mines called Poulton quarries.   23 large mine (The Tump).   24 large mine, Westwood.   25 mine, Longsplatt quarry.   26 mine, Kingsdown quarry.   27 the largest mine, Farleigh Down stone, with 28.   28 South Farleigh, mine, Farleigh Down stone (Outstone).   29 only open one in Box area (Hazelbury).   30 Clift (formerly Stone's quarries).   31 No. 4 Box (adj. No 4 shaft Box tunnel) (Stone's quarries).   32 Tyning (= Tennis Court) (later Clift).   33 No. 6 Box (Clift).   34 Lower Hill Box.   35 Hartham No. 2.   36 Hartham No. 1 (also known as Pickwick).   37 Corsham Down quarry, mine, opened about 1845 (Spring).   38 Huddswell.   39 Stone's No. 6 Corsham.   40 Pictor's No. 6 Corsham.   41 No. 7 Corsham, Spring or Waterhole.   42 Sands or Westwells.   43 Monks Park Northern (Sumsion's Monks; the present Monks Park Mine).   44 Eastern Monks Park (Pictor's Monks or Eastleys).   45 Western Monks Park (The Ridge).   46 Ridge (Old Ridge).   47 Park Lane.   48 Old workings at Bathampton from which enormous quantities have been extracted (open works with incline to canal, probably date therefore from early 19th cent.).

15

at Hartham Park in late 1945. The most significant development underground was the testing of Samson coal cutters at Moor Park in 1948, machines which are still used in the surviving underground quarries Monks Park and Westwood. The record of these post-war changes, of the past and present of Bath Stone mining, forms the subject of our illustrations.

KEY TO THE ILLUSTRATIONS

WINNING STONE BY HAND—THE OLD METHOD OF WORKING
(Figures 4–19)

OTHER ASPECTS
(Figures 20–25)

SURFACE TRANSPORT
(Figures 26–32)

MODERN WORKING
(Figures 33–38)

NATURAL HISTORY IN THE MINES
(Figures 39–41)

Fig. 4. Picking the breach. Picking out the bed beneath the roof to a depth of 5 feet. The work commences with a 3ft shaft pick and ends with one of 6ft shaft. Working by the light of a single oil lamp, to the left of the pick head. Hartham Park, 1947.

Fig. 5. Sawyers cutting out the first stone from the breach, known as the wrist stone, using 6ft saws and water to wash out the stone dust. Hartham Park, 1947.

Fig. 6. Making the back cut after the removal of the wrist stone. The shallow bladed 'razzer' is used until the cut is deep enough to take the full sized saw (frig bob). Hartham Park, 1947.

Fig. 7. Cutting out the bottom bed with 7ft saws. A natural joint at the rear meant that no back cut was needed on that occasion. Monks Park.

Fig. 8. Cutting out the bottom bed and making a back cut. Note how the man making the back cut has reversed his saw, backing it against a piece of rail held between his feet. The picker is testing the stone for natural faults. Note the drip can and the three small oil lamps. Monks Park, about 1930.

Fig. 9. Pillars left to support the roof demonstrate the pick marks and the successive saw cuts. By setting the outer cuts at an angle the sawyers could obtain larger blocks from the lower beds. Downward tapering pillars resulted, a feature of the hand-worked mines. Monks Park.

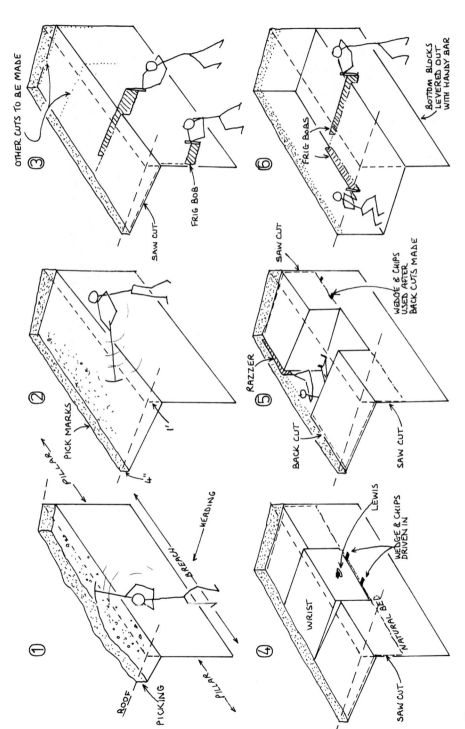

Fig. 10. A diagrammatic summary of the stages in hand-working.

Fig. 11 Lifting out a block of the bottom bed by means of the lewis pins attached to it. Monks Park, about the beginning of the century.

Fig. 12. Scappling a block with the stone axe. The rough end is being sawn off another. The lewis is clearly shown again. Monks Park, at the beginning of the century.

Fig. 13. Loading stone onto a trolley to be sent to the surface. Small pieces of stone (squats) between the block and the trolley allowed movement and prevented the derailment of the trolley. Moor Park, 1946.

Fig. 14. Hauliers and horse drawing a load of block from the heading to the bottom of the shaft. Park Lane, 1948.

Fig. 15. Blocks ascending the slope shaft to the surface 90ft above. The shaft has a 1 in 2 slope and the only means of entry on foot, involving 212 steps. Monks Park.

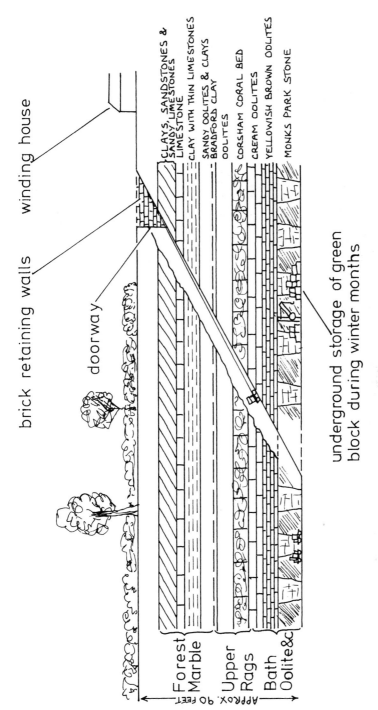

brick retaining walls

winding house

doorway

underground storage of green block during winter months

CLAYS, SANDSTONES & SANDY LIMESTONES
LIMESTONE
CLAY WITH THIN LIMESTONES
SANDY OOLITES & CLAYS
BRADFORD CLAY
OOLITES
CORSHAM CORAL BED
CREAM OOLITES
YELLOWISH BROWN OOLITES
MONKS PARK STONE

Forest Marble
Upper Rags
Bath Oolite &c

APPROX. 90 FEET

Fig. 16.   Section through a mine showing the slope shaft.

Fig. 17. Horse drawn haulage from the top of the slope shaft to the stacking ground. Park Lane about the beginning of the century.

Fig. 18. Stacking the block at the surface, by means of a hand gantry. Monks Park, 1930.

Fig. 19. Another surface stacking gang, this time using a crane.

Fig. 20. A sawyer cutting slabs from a large block of stone at a mason's yard. Note the traditional one-legged stool. Station Yard, Corsham, about 1948.

Local variety names which have been used for Bath Stone:

Box Corngrit
Box Ground
Box Scallett
Combe Down
Corngrit
Corsham
Corsham Blue
Corsham Down (Upper Bed and
    Bottom Bed)
Farleigh Down
Hartham Park Corsham
Hartham Park Ground
Hazelbury
Kingsdown
Monks Park
Odd Down
Park Lane
Ridge
Stoke Ground
Westwood Ground
Winsley Ground

Fig. 21. A wooden tub completely encrusted in calcium carbonate in the 26 years since it was placed to catch dripping water for the horse to drink. Monks Park, 1978. History does not record what happened to the inner workings of the horse.

Fig. 22. A hauliers drawing at the bottom of the Monks Park slope shaft of Punch, the last horse to work in the stone mines, 1952. The mines are full of graffiti, dates of working, records of historic events, comments on work-mates, &c.

Fig. 23. A horse being brought to the surface to be shod or to the main stables for the weekend. Park Lane, about the beginning of the century.

Fig. 24. Quarrymen at the surface with all the tools required to mine the stone. Note the stencil on the blocks is BS (Bath Stone) Firms.

Fig. 25. Tools from the days of handworking in the former underground museum at Monks Park. Note the trade mark stencil of the former St. Aldhelm quarry with its gauntlet recalling the legend of the discovery of Box Stone.

Fig. 26. Hauling block from the mine stacking ground to the main line railway wharf. Monks Park, 1934.

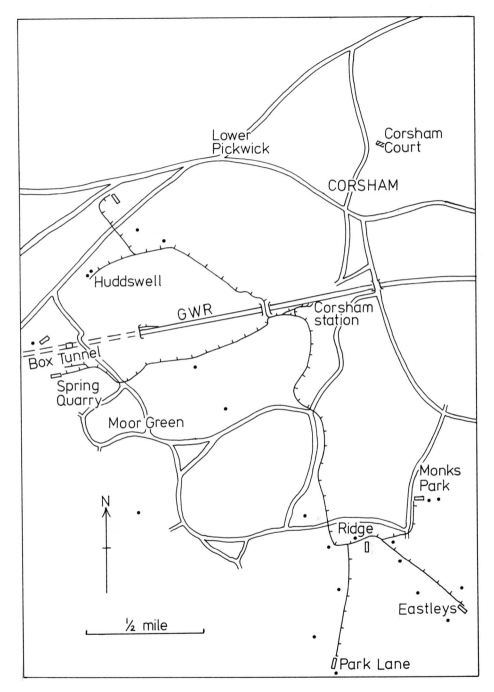

Fig. 27. Map of the quarry railways in the Corsham district, about 1890.

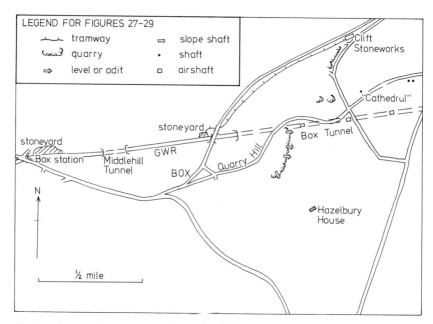

Fig. 28. Map of the quarry railways in the Box district, about 1890.

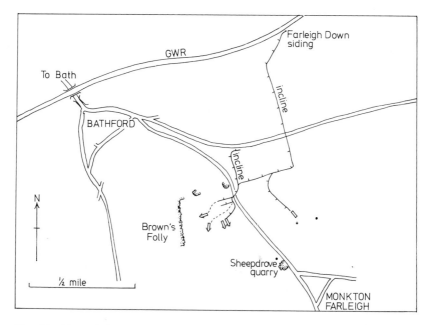

Fig. 29. Map of the quarry railways and inclines in the Farleigh Down district, about 1890.

THE QUARRY TRAMWAYS

by David Pollard

The increased quarrying of stone in the eighteenth and nineteenth centuries led to the construction of railways and tramways to carry stone from the quarries to wharves on the River Avon, the Kennet and Avon Canal or the Great Western Railway.

All the tramways ran downhill to the wharves, the loaded trolleys descending by gravity. In some cases the trolleys were controlled by a brakeman and the empty ones returned by horsepower, in others the tramway had a double tracked incline whereby the load trolley descending at the end of a rope would pull empty trolleys up the other track.

The first recorded tramway was built in 1730 to the design of John Padmore, a Bristol engineer, connecting Ralph Allen's Combe Down quarries with Dolemeads Wharf on the River Avon about a mile and a half away. The rails were made of oak scantlings about six inches by five inches in section and laid to a gauge of 3ft 9in. Although very successful, it was dismantled shortly after Ralph Allen's death in 1764.

The making of the Kennet and Avon Canal in 1794–1810 stimulated the building of three tramways. The Conkwell and Murhill lines were made to carry stone used in the construction of the canal, although the latter remained in use for many years. It was of nominal 4ft gauge using cast iron fish belly rails seated in chairs on stone sleeper blocks. The Hampton Down line of 1808 ran down to the canal near Holcombe Farm by means of two inclines. Its trolleys had flangeless wheels which ran in L section rails fixed to stone sleeper blocks.

Underground tramways were in use in the Corsham area before 1862 and in 1876 the Board of Trade sanctioned three surface tramways of 2ft 5½in gauge to link Hudswell, Westwells and Ridge quarries with Corsham Station (G.W.R.). At a later date Monks Park and other quarries were connected to the system. The Corsham quarries were entered by steeply inclined tunnels known as slope shafts, up which trolleys were drawn by a cable powered by a steam engine or electric winch.

On December 3rd, 1877 the 2ft 5½in gauge Westwood quarry tramway was opened down to the Avoncliff siding of the Great Western Railway via a double tracked incline. Its trolleys were very squat due to the low ceiling within the quarry. Other quarry tramways were at Limpley Stoke, Monkton Farleigh and Clift quarry at Box. The latter was notable for its use of a steam locomotive underground.

The only remaining tramway and slope shaft is at Monks Park quarry although horses have of course given way to locomotives, diesel on the surface and battery electric underground.

Fig. 30. The stone wharf at Corsham Station (G.W.R.) Notice the company names on the trucks and the loading by means of a hand crane.

Fig. 31. The eastern portal of Box Tunnel with the quarry railway tunnel into one of the many stone mines in the district visible to the right.

CORSHAM DOWN QUARRY, EAST END OF BOX TUNNEL.

To Randell & Saunders,

Quarrymen & Stone Merchants.

Fig. 32. A quarry company bill head, also showing the eastern end of Box Tunnel. Horses drawing a load of stone can be seen passing over the tunnel portal.

1887 Formation of the Bath Stone Firms Limited.

1908 Formation of the Bath & Portland Stone Firms Limited.

1960 Formation of the Bath & Portland Group, a holding company, following diversification of the activities of the above company.

Kingston Minerals is the quarrying division of the Bath & Portland Group Limited whose interests include building, civil engineering, agriculture and light engineering.

Kingston Minerals operate from about 40 locations spread over Wales, Southwest and Northwest England and the Midlands. The main stone producing works still in use are Monk's Park and Westwood mines (Bath Stone), Guiting (Guiting Stone from the Inferior Oolite), Doulting near Shepton Mallet (Doulting Stone from the Inferior Oolite) and the Isle of Portland, Dorset (Portland Stone).

Fig. 33. A Samson coal cutting machine making the horizontal cut known as the picking cut. Notice that the automatic jacks of the machine are extended and it is also ramped up on timbers to gain sufficient height to hug the ceiling.

Fig. 34. Samson coal cutting machine making a vertical cut. The pillar on the right shows the typical Samson cut marks.

Fig. 35. All the cuts in the breach completed and the wrist stone removed. Note the wedge and chips inserted on the natural bed of the centre block, ready to be driven in by sledge hammer and thus lift the upper part up off its natural bed. Westwood Mine.

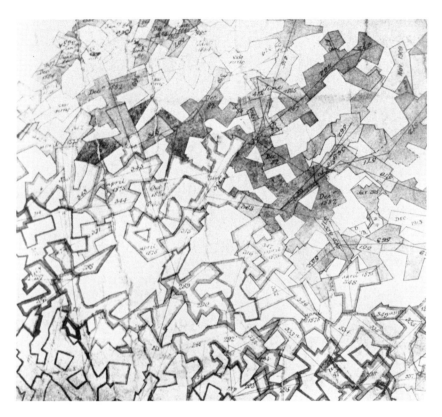

Fig. 36. A quarry map, recording workings going back to 1872. The dates of working are entered in each section. The size of the pillars left may illustrate the state of the roof in that area or the quality of the stone.

Fig. 37. Old workings in the Clift Mine, known as 'The Cathedral' owing to the unusual height of the ceiling. Blocks were hauled up through the shaft. Its edges have been notched by the haulage cables.

Fig. 38. Old underground workings being used as a factory during the 1939–1945 war.

Some dates of closure:

Clift	1968
Copenacre	1937 (also known as Cob, Cobenacre)
Hartham Park	1964
Huddswell	1914
Monks	1937 (Pictor's Monks or Eastleys)
Park Lane	1958
Ridge	1914
Sands	1937
Seven Shaft	1914
Spring	1937
Westwell	1952 (also known as Moor Park)

Note the marked groupings with the two periods of requisition by H.M. Government.

Fig. 39. Bats are common visitors to the mines, sometimes already carrying identification rings. Rhinolophus equinum.

BATHYNELLA CHAPPUISI.

Fig. 40. Bathynella chappuisi. Discovered by A. G. Lowndes, MA, FLS in 1927 but not identified until 1931. About 1 mm long, it was found in a water tub in an underground working and was not recorded again for nearly 30 years.

Fig. 41. Coprinus fungi growing by old rails. The spore was probably brought in on miners' boots. Various types of fungi are quite common in the old workings, especially on old pit props.

GLOSSARY OF STONE MINERS' TERMS

Ball horseshoe-shaped iron piece attached to the lewis pin.

Breach the width worked between two pillars, removed first by the picker.

Brog nail used to fix rails down to wooden sleepers.

Brogging hammer for nailing brogs into the sleepers.

Callust calcite coating deposited by water underground, i.e. flowstone.

Cant a long end on a block of stone.

Cap flat piece of wood at top of a prop between it and roof.

Chaps brown threads running about six inches into the stone.

Chips two flat pieces of metal inserted with the wedge, see below, when lifting block from its natural bed.

Chog metal sleeve in centre of wood block in ceiling to take the pin from the upright of a hand crane.

Chog hole square hole in roof for hand crane; 12 inches square by 10 inches deep.

Cleats oak wedges placed in roof joints. In the event of movement these would lock the roof blocks before they could fall.

Cockle calcite crystals in a hole in the stone.

Crab like a boatman's winch. Used with a lewis and pulley block in the roof to haul hand cranes up into position.

Cricks brown faults going through the stone, usually iron minerals washed in.

Crane cup iron cup in the centre of a crane stone.

Crane stone square hole in floor for the upright of a hand crane to stand in.

Drip tin can with hole and matchstick in, to drip feed water into saw cut.

Frig bob wide bladed saw used to cut out the blocks.

Ginny ring see Whim.

Gobs small pieces of stone.

Green block unhardened fresh stone which still has its quarry sap, see below.

Hand crane worked by four men, two on each side. Capable of lifting 5 tons.

Handy bar worked by two or three men, a large crow-bar used to lift bottom stones off their bed.

Hatching The offset along a pillar between one saw cut and the next.

Heading a working face.

Holing iron a short iron with a chisel head used to complete lewis holes.

Jadding iron long iron rod used to take out the back corners of the breach which could not be reached by the curving swing of the pick. A good picker would not need to use one as he would be able to swing both to right and left.

Jim crow tool to bend or straighten tramway rails.

Jump a change in level of the beds, i.e. a geological fault.

Kivel the trade mark of Kingston Minerals, a tool with a hammer head opposite a pick head, used in squaring up harder stones, e.g. Portland, but not on Bath Stone which is softer at the time of extraction, hardening on exposure.

Lewis trapezoid shaped attachment in three sections, inserted into tapered holes made in blocks to enable them to be pulled from the face or lifted.

Muck box three sided metal container for haulage of rubble.

Nips small version of shears, see below.

Old men brown faults in all directions.

Opening hammer used to set the teeth of saws.

Paddy link link similar in shape to a key-hole, used to make a loop on a chain and hold it without tying.

Pick Beater pick, for packing sleepers under rails. Holing pick, for making holes for the chips and wedge and commencing lewis holes. Muck or navvy pick, for breaking up hard rubble. Picking pick, for picking out the roof area before sawing the stone. Roughing pick, for squaring up the block before finishing with a double-headed axe.

Picking the bed to be removed at the top.

Pillar area of stone left to support the roof.

Point small iron tool for breaking gobs.

Quarry sap natural moisture in the stone when in the ground.

Razzer tapering saw used to commence cutting until the frig bob could be inserted.

Samson Mavor & Coulson arc wall shearer.

Saw block block with long slot in used to hold saws while sharpening and re-setting.

Scappled block block which has been roughly squared up by hand axe.

Scorter diagonal wooden prop from pillar to roof.

Scriber tool to scratch number and cubic size on block.

Shears like large calipers, used for lifting block.

Sleighter joint a clean fault in the stone.

Squats small stones, one in front and two at the back, put on the trolley before the block is put on it. The squats allow the trolley to rock on bends in the mine roadways. If it were rigid it would derail.

Tapper pebble or piece of metal used to test stone by striking it and listening to the ring. Faults invisible to the eye can thus be traced.

Trace chain used to pull block from face instead of a lewis.

Trolley mine wagon, sometimes called a bogey.

Trolley bar bar to stop a trolley or to replace it on the rails.

Wedge short broad chisel driven in between the chips, see above.

Whim animal powered winding drum or winch.

Whimmer like a long brace and bit, used for making blast holes in the days when black powder (gunpowder) was used.

Windy drill pneumatic drill.

Wood hole a piece of fossil driftwood in the bed.

Wrist first block removed from the heading after making a new set of cuts. The wrist had to be wedged off from the back and when it had been removed a sawyer could squeeze into the narrow space and make back-cuts behind the other blocks.

THE STONEMINERS

Chopper man who squared up (scappled) the stone using a hand axe.

Dayman member of the stacking gang in the stock yard.

Ganger man responsible for the heading.

Picker man who removed the roof bed, using picks with increasing length of handle.

Roadman maintained the roadways in the mine.

Sawyer man who sawed out the blocks. By putting the saws in at an angle on the outer margins of the heading, the sawyer could increase the width of the lower blocks over the size for which the picker had been paid in removing the roof bed. This was known as robbing the picker. It resulted in a downward tapering shape to the pillars left in the mines to support the roof.

References

Anon. Box Hill and Its Bath Stone Quarries, *The Builder*, **20** (1862) 613–15.

Anon. Building Stone from Underground, *Quarry Managers' Journal*, **46** (1962) 175–84.

Anon. *A Guide to the History and Geology of Bath Stone* (Kingston Minerals, 1970).

Anon. *Bath Oolite Series*, 4pp foolscap (Kingston Minerals, n.d.).

Anon. *The Bath Stone Quarries*, 7pp (Bath & Portland Stone Firms, n.d.).

Cotterell, T. Sturge, Bath Stone, *61st Congress British Archaeological Assoc.* (Bath, 1904).

Elton, A. Early Stone Railways in the Bath Area, from The Prehistory of Railways, *Proc. Somerset Archaeological & Nat. Hist. Soc.*, **107** (1963) 31–59.

Green, G. W. and Donovan, D. T. The Great Oolite of the Bath Area, *Bull. Geol. Surv. G.B.* **30** (1969) 1–64.

Haddon, J. *Bath* (Batsford, 1973).

(Harris, G. F.) Bath Stone, *The Builder*, **68** (1895) 273–78.

(Harris, G. F.) Bath Stone 2, *The Builder*, **69** (1895) 291–95.

Little, Bryan, *Prior Park, Its History & Description* (Prior Park College, 1975).

Rowe, Rev. J. Tetley, A Block of Bath Stone, *Church Monthly* (1902) 90–93.

Tucker, R. J. Box Quarries, Wiltshire, *Industrial Archaeology*, **5** (1968) 178–83.

Tucker, R. J., Bater, R. J. and Mansfield, R. W. Box Stone Mines, *Mem. Cotham Spelaeological Soc.* **4** (1968–69) 9–29.

Weaver, Paul, The Box and Corsham Quarry & Munitions Tramways, *Gearwheel* (1975) 5pp, N. Wilts & S. Gloucs. Preservation Soc.

Wright, Reginald M. W. *Bath Abbey* (Pitkin Pictorials, 1973).

Anon. Box Tunnel, *Great Western Railway Magazine*, **40** (1928) 356ff.

Acknowledgements

The authors wish to thank Kingston Minerals Limited for their permission to publish company copyright photographs.

54